Sir Isaac Newton

Anita Croy

CRABTREE
PUBLISHING COMPANY
WWW.CRABTREEBOOKS.COM

CRABTREE
PUBLISHING COMPANY
WWW.CRABTREEBOOKS.COM

Author: Anita Croy
Editors: Sarah Eason, Melissa Boyd, Ellen Rodger
Proofreader and indexer: Jennifer Sanderson
Proofreader: Wendy Scavuzzo
Editorial director: Kathy Middleton
Design: Paul Myerscough and Lynne Lennon
Photo research: Rachel Blount
Print coordinator: Katherine Berti

Written, developed, and produced by Calcium

Photo Credits:
t=Top, c=Center, b=Bottom, l= Left, r=Right

Inside: Shutterstock: 360b: p. 59r; Agsandrew: p. 52;
Ansharphoto: p. 48; Uwe Aranas: p. 55; Aspen Photo:
p. 37t; Tony Baggett: p. 42; El Basker: p. 45t; Bedrin: p. 58;
Bikeworldtravel: p. 61b; Cgterminal: pp. 20tr, 20br, 21bl;
Andrea Danti: p. 25; Dark Moon Pictures: p. 35c; DavidYoung:
p. 9t; designer_an: p. 41b; EngravingFactory: p. 35t; Everett
Historical: p. 24; Christos Georghiou: p. 32; Helioscribe:
p. 34; Mark Herreid: p. 29t; Ilkercelik: p. 37b; Jorisvo: pp. 39,
41t; Georgios Kollidas: p. 21t; Leonrwoods: p. 8; Master-L:
p. 57b; Mattxfoto: p. 7c; Anamaria Mejia: p. 17t; Aksenova
Natalya: p. 19; Natata: p. 7bl; Nicku: p. 49c; Mike Pellinni:
p. 22; Pikepicture: p. 31b; Pisaphotography: p. 45c;
Purematterian: p. 29b; R Martin Seddon: pp. 6, 60; Elena
Sherengovskaya: p. 11c; Ververidis Vasilis: p. 15t; Vesnation:
p. 17b; Wellcome Collection: Robert Hooke/Wellcome
Collection CC BY: p. 50; Godfrey Kneller/Wellcome Collection
CC BY: p. 51t; Numlx: p. 20; R. Page after Sir G. Kneller/
Wellcome Collection CC BY: p. 4; J. Quartley after J.M.L.R./
Wellcome Collection CC BY: p. 27; Wikimedia Commons:
p. 57t; Aristotle: p. 9b; William Blake: p. 38; R. Earlom after
D. Loggan/Wellcome Images: p. 11t; Caspar David Friedrich:
p. 56; Galileo: p. 14; Justus van Gent: p. 28; Robert Hooke/
Wellcome Images: pp. 21b, 31t; Jean-Pierre Houël: p. 54; Paul
Mellon Collection in the Yale Center for British Art: p. 47;
Thomas Murray: p. 36; NASA, ESA, and the Hubble Heritage
Team (STScI/AURA)-ESA/Hubble Collaboration: p. 51b; Isaac
Newton: p. 40; Adriaen van Ostade: p. 46; Sage Ross: p. 12;
Jan Baptist Weenix: p. 18; Wellcome Images: pp. 10, 15c, 30;
John Michael Wright: p. 26; X-ray (NASA/CXC/SAO); optical
(NASA/HST); radio: (ACTA): p. 16.

Library and Archives Canada Cataloguing in Publication

Title: Sir Isaac Newton / Anita Croy.
Names: Croy, Anita, author.
Description: Series statement: Scientists who changed the world |
   Includes index.
Identifiers: Canadiana (print) 20200226142 |
   Canadiana (ebook) 20200226169 |
   ISBN 9780778782216 (hardcover) |
   ISBN 9780778782278 (softcover) |
   ISBN 9781427126139 (HTML)
Subjects: LCSH: Newton, Isaac, 1642-1727—Juvenile literature. |
   LCSH: Physicists—Biography—Juvenile literature. |
   LCGFT: Biographies.
Classification: LCC QC16.N7 C76 2021 | DDC j530.092—dc23

Library of Congress Cataloging-in-Publication Data

Names: Croy, Anita, author.
Title: Sir Isaac Newton / Anita Croy.
Description: New York : Crabtree Publishing Company, 2021. |
   Series: Scientists who changed the world | Includes index.
Identifiers: LCCN 2020017171 (print) |
   LCCN 2020017172 (ebook) |
   ISBN 9780778782216 (hardcover) |
   ISBN 9780778782278 (paperback) |
   ISBN 9781427126139 (ebook)
Subjects: LCSH: Newton, Isaac, 1642-1727--Juvenile literature. |
   Physicists--Great Britain--Biography--Juvenile literature.
Classification: LCC QC16.N7 C79 2021 (print) |
   LCC QC16.N7 (ebook) | DDC 530.092 [B]--dc23
LC record available at https://lccn.loc.gov/2020017171
LC ebook record available at https://lccn.loc.gov/2020017172

Crabtree Publishing Company
www.crabtreebooks.com   1-800-387-7650

Printed in the U.S.A./082020/CG20200601

Published in Canada
Crabtree Publishing
616 Welland Ave.
St. Catharines, Ontario
L2M 5V6

Published in the United States
Crabtree Publishing
347 Fifth Ave
Suite 1402-145
New York, NY 10016

Published in the United Kingdom
Crabtree Publishing
Maritime House
Basin Road North, Hove
BN41 1WR

Published in Australia
Crabtree Publishing
3 Charles Street
Coburg North
VIC, 3058

Contents

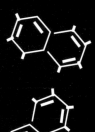

This portrait shows Sir Isaac Newton in 1702. He is wearing a wig, which was the fashion at the time.

SIR ISAAC NEWTON
Biography

Born: December 25, 1642

Place of birth: Woolsthorpe, Lincolnshire, England

Mother: Hannah Ayscough

Father: Isaac Newton

Famous for: Creating the foundations for modern science and our understanding of how the universe works due to a remarkable range of discoveries.

How he changed the world: Newton discovered **gravity**, wrote the three Laws of Motion that form the basis of modern **physics**, and figured out a new type of math, called **calculus**.

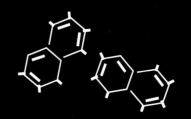

Newton said that his major CONTRIBUTION to improving our KNOWLEDGE of the world was his ability to be PATIENT and think things through SLOWLY and THOROUGHLY.

Js.° Newton°

VILLAGE BOY

Isaac Newton was born on Christmas Day in 1642. He was born early, and so tiny that no one expected him to survive. His mother thought that baby Isaac would die, just as Isaac's father had done three months earlier. Isaac Newton senior had been a wealthy local farmer, but like many other men of his class, he could not read or write.

When Isaac was three years old, his mother remarried. His stepfather did not like Isaac, who was sent to live with his grandparents. From that day until he was 10, he hardly saw his mother. He missed her so much that sometimes he would climb a tree and gaze at the house where she and her new family lived.

Newton's family home in Woolsthorpe, England, looks much like it did in the 1600s.

Isaac…hardly saw his mother. He missed her so much…

When Isaac's stepfather died, his mother came with his three half-siblings to live with Isaac and her parents. She brought a lot of books with her. Isaac had learned to read in his village school and now had many books to choose from. There was even a notebook, which Isaac used to write down all his ideas. When he was 12, his mother sent him to King's School in Grantham, so he could learn enough to be a successful farmer. The school was 6 miles (9.6 km) away, so Isaac lived with a family in the town.

Ideas that changed the world

Newton later wrote:"I do not know what I may appear to the world, but to myself I seem to have been only like a boy playing on the seashore, and diverting myself in now and then finding a smoother pebble or a prettier shell than ordinary, whilst the great ocean of truth lay all undiscovered before me."

Exploring the ideas

Newton always knew he was unusual. He thought that what made him different was that he was distracted by little things rather than trying to answer huge questions, such as how the universe came into being. Yet, by concentrating on tiny details, he came to understand that they could be the key to unlocking much greater ideas or truths.

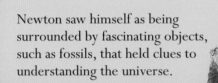

Newton saw himself as being surrounded by fascinating objects, such as fossils, that held clues to understanding the universe.

HISTORY'S STORY

Only boys from better-off families went to King's School because they had to pay fees. If girls had any education, they were taught at home. At King's School, lessons were taught in Latin. Math was not seen as important, so Isaac only learned basic arithmetic. He also studied Greek so he could read the works of ancient scholars such as Aristotle and Plato.

SHEEP OR STUDIES?

By the time Newton finished at King's School, he was head boy—a sort of "class president." But he almost did not finish school at all. His mother often took him out of school to work on her land, but it was clear that Newton was more interested in books than farming. One day, the sheep escaped into a neighbor's field while he read. They ate all the crops and his mother was fined. Newton was soon back at school.

For much of his school days, Newton's grades were poor. Only when he decided to work hard and apply himself did he go to the top of his class. His headmaster, Mr. Stokes, realized that Newton was very smart, and offered to let him study for free. Stokes and Newton's uncle, William Ayscough, could see that the boy needed to continue his studies. They wanted him to go to Cambridge University.

Stokes prepared Newton for his university entrance examinations and, at the age of 18, Newton won a place at Trinity College, Cambridge. At first, he had to work to pay his fees, but he later won a scholarship, which meant everything was paid for. Today, Cambridge is one of the world's leading universities. But when Newton started there in 1661, it was not as forward-thinking as some other European universities.

In the 1600s, the English economy was dominated by wool taken from the millions of sheep raised on farmland there.

The old order

Newton studied Aristotle (384–322 B.C.E.) and other Greek scholars. Aristotle believed that Earth was at the center of the universe and that everything moved around it, including the Sun. The Catholic Church, which in Newton's time was the most powerful organization in Europe, supported Aristotle's view of the universe. The church taught that God controlled everything, and kept the universe in constant motion.

Challenging ideas

Newton lived at a time when European **astronomers** were openly challenging Aristotle's ideas. They believed that Earth **orbited** the Sun, not the other way around. Scientists such as Nicolaus Copernicus (1473–1543), Tycho Brahe (1546–1601), Johannes Kepler (1571–1630), and Galileo Galilei (1564–1642) had all suggested that the Sun was at the center of the universe.

These ideas attracted Newton, who was bored with his studies in **geometry** and **algebra**. He started to work on a type of math he called "analytical geometry." He was also interested in **mechanical philosophy**, which defined the universe as a vast and complex machine in which all the separate parts worked together.

At first, Newton paid for his studies at Trinity College, Cambridge, by acting as a servant to his wealthier fellow students.

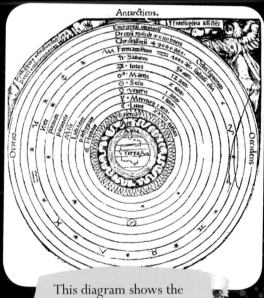

This diagram shows the universe as described by Aristotle, with the Sun, moon, and planets orbiting Earth.

9

THE PLAGUE

By 1665, Newton had finished his **undergraduate** studies and was on his way to earning a master's degree—but no one yet recognized him as a genius. His grades were not great but he had done enough to become a "scholar." Scholars had privileges such as better places to live and having their tuition paid. Suddenly, however, his studies came to a halt when the university was shut.

A body collector calls "bring out your dead" to collect and remove the bodies of **plague** victims in London.

In London, people began to die in large numbers from a deadly disease called plague. The plague was highly **contagious** and had no known cure. It struck England several times during the 1600s.

Cambridge sent all its students home in the hope that they would not be infected. Newton went back to his mother's house in Woolsthorpe. There, he had the time to think. He started to work more seriously on his ideas. One thing he thought about was a new kind of math. Math could already describe how fast a wagon was going, for example, but what about an object that traveled at different speeds and in different directions on its journey? Newton invented a math to describe things that change constantly. He called the method **"fluxions."** Today, it is known as calculus. Other areas Newton investigated while at home were the nature of light and color, and the force that made things fall to Earth.

A new math

Newton stayed at home until the plague finally ended in 1667. During his "vacation," he had made many important discoveries. Back in Cambridge, one of his professors, Isaac Barrow (1630–1677), persuaded him to share his ideas about fluxions. Barrow was the most senior professor of math at Cambridge. Reluctantly, Newton agreed to let his findings be published. His system was greeted with great excitement. When Barrow left the university in 1669, he arranged for Newton to have his job. Newton was now a professor of math at Cambridge University!

Isaac Barrow was an exceptional mathematician, as well as a kind friend to Newton.

Plague traveled easily in the 1600s because black rats were everywhere and moved around England, hidden in cargoes of food.

HISTORY'S STORY

When the plague arrived in England, nobody knew what caused it. We now know it was caused by **bacteria** carried on fleas that lived on black rats. In just 18 months, the plague killed around 100,000 people in London—nearly one-quarter of the city's population. Places where people gathered, such as schools and theaters, closed to prevent the spread of the disease.

CHAPTER 2

This orrery, a model of the universe showing the orbits of the planets, was made in 1767.

THE AGE OF REASON
Background

Name: The Age of Reason, also known as the Enlightenment

Definition: A movement led by scholars and scientists that emphasized reason, the individual, and questioning of established views. The movement was philosophical, or concerned with questioning ideas about reality and the universe.

Started: Many historians say the movement began in 1637, when the French philosopher René Descartes stated: "I think, therefore I am."

Ended: Around 1800

Location: Initially Europe, then America

Areas of interest: Philosophy, math, astronomy, **optics**, mechanical philosophy

Newton once wrote that his DISCOVERIES were only possible because he had STOOD on the shoulders of GIANTS.

THE SCIENTIFIC METHOD

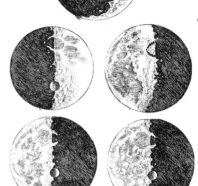

Newton was the greatest scientist since Galileo Galilei, who died less than a year before Newton's birth. Newton was able to build on the new approach to science introduced by Galileo and others. Before Galileo, most scientists built their observations around the teachings of Aristotle and the Catholic Church. Galileo refused to do that.

Galileo made careful sketches of what he saw on the Moon, including its rough surface.

When Galileo used the telescope he had invented to look at the moon, he made a remarkable discovery. Aristotle had believed that the heavens were without flaw, but Galileo could see that the moon was not a smooth, perfect circle, as Aristotle had described. Galileo could clearly see that the moon's surface was rough and had mountains and craters. He realized he had made an important discovery.

Galileo also used a new approach to scientific discovery. He decided that every experiment he made had to be tested and retested. Instead of fitting his experiments into existing ideas, Galileo came up with an explanation, called a **hypothesis**, to make sense of the results of his experiments. Then he carried out more experiments to test his ideas until the hypothesis was proven. Only then did he write up his **conclusion**. This is the scientific method all scientists follow today.

Ideas that changed the world

One day, Newton wrote a Latin phrase in his notebook. Translated into English, it means: "Plato is my friend, Aristotle is my friend, but my greatest friend is truth."

Exploring the ideas

What Newton meant was that he enjoyed studying the ancient Greeks and their ideas about how the universe worked. These were still widely taught in universities. However, he was not prepared to accept that what they had written nearly 2,000 years earlier was correct. He believed, like Galileo, that every idea had to be challenged. If he observed something that did not agree with ancient ideas, he was prepared to say so and to show how the old ideas were wrong.

Aristotle shaped European thinking in the period after the fall of the Roman Empire in 476 C.E.

At his trial, Galileo (kneeling) was forced to withdraw his theory.

HISTORY'S STORY

Galileo's work brought him into conflict with the Catholic Church. The Church said that, by insisting that Earth orbited the Sun, Galileo was guilty of heresy, or dangerous ideas that contradicted the Church. Galileo was tried by the Inquisition, a Church court, and found guilty of heresy. He was placed under **house arrest** for the rest of his life.

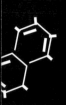

SHAPE OF THE UNIVERSE

In 1543, a Polish monk and scientist named Nicolaus Copernicus said that Aristotle and the Catholic Church were wrong: Earth was not the center of the universe; the Sun was. Copernicus could not conclusively prove his idea, but his work got other scientists thinking.

According to Aristotle and the Church, everything beyond the moon was fixed and unchanging.

Later that century, a Danish astronomer named Tycho Brahe built the best **observatory** in Europe. He spent thousands of hours studying the positions of planets and stars with the latest equipment. In November 1572, Brahe observed a supernova caused by the explosion of a giant, dying star and realized that it lay far beyond the moon. According to Aristotle and the Church, everything beyond the moon was fixed and unchanging—but the supernova contradicted, or disagreed with, their ideas.

This cloud of gas is what remains of the supernova seen by Tycho Brahe nearly 500 years ago.

Brahe suggested that, while the whole universe circled Earth, the other planets circled the Sun. While this theory was later proven wrong, Brahe was one of the first people to realize that the universe is not fixed but in constant motion.

Kepler's breakthrough

After Brahe's death in 1601, his student Johannes Kepler went back over all of Brahe's observations. Like Brahe, he assumed that the planets orbited in perfect circles, but when he studied the **data**, Kepler made a startling discovery. He realized that Mars travels in a slightly flattened orbit that is more like an oval than a circle. When Kepler published his findings in 1609, many astronomers paid no attention because the findings went against accepted ideas.

The Sun's "movement"

The discoveries made by many astronomers in the 1500s and 1600s directly contradicted the teachings of the Catholic Church. They also seemed to go against common sense. When people looked at the skies, they saw that the Sun rose every morning and set every evening. It seemed clear that the Sun orbited Earth. When Newton was born in 1642, this was still accepted by many people. People used the Sun to tell the time using sundials, which threw a shadow to track the Sun's movement through the sky. As a boy, Newton made his own sundial to track the path of sunlight on a wall of his home.

This statue celebrates the achievements of Tycho Brahe (left) and Johannes Kepler.

Before clocks, sundials were accurate enough for people to tell the time.

I THINK...

When Newton was at Cambridge University, the most exciting and famous philosopher in Europe was a Frenchman. René Descartes (1596–1650) challenged the ancient view of the world with his ideas. Now seen as the founder of modern philosophy, Descartes laid the foundations on which Newton developed his ideas.

Descartes studied philosophy, math, and **natural philosophy**, an old term used to describe the study of nature and the universe. His starting point was to doubt everything he had ever learned, then to figure out what he was able to know with absolute certainty. He soon realized that the only thing he knew was that he existed because, as he said, "I think, therefore I am." He reasoned that, because he could think, he must exist. By the same **logic**, God and the teachings of the Church could not be proven to exist beyond doubt.

"I think, therefore I am."

Descartes tried to develop a **fundamental** set of principles, or ideas, that could be said to be true without any doubt. A scientist at heart, he called his method "methodical skepticism." It basically meant that any idea that can be doubted is false. To prove something, one must use the principles of deduction, or logically following basic laws.

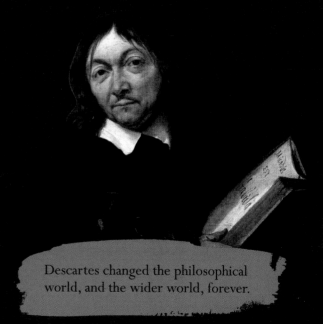

Descartes changed the philosophical world, and the wider world, forever.

Looking for laws

Descartes thought that the physical world was made up of invisible, moving **particles** of **matter**, surrounded by an invisible substance called ether. In his belief, the **interactions** between these particles explained everything in nature. He thought that the world could be understood by mathematical **equations** that would explain the laws of how things behaved. He called his approach "experimental philosophy." Descartes preferred math to philosophy because he believed it was based on undeniable truths, such as the rules of geometry. The problem with philosophy was that, for every argument, there was an argument to prove it wrong.

The wax problem

Descartes believed that the human senses could not always be trusted. He took a piece of wax as his example. When it is cold, wax looks and appears different from wax that is melted—yet both are the same substance. Descartes reasoned that our senses can only tell us how a thing appears and not about its true nature. To truly know about an object meant relying on reason, he argued.

Descartes wondered how it was possible to tell anything about the reality of existence when it was impossible to understand even wax.

HISTORY'S STORY

Robert Boyle (1627–1691) was one of Newton's few long-term friends. He is now seen as the father of **chemistry**, which was then developing into a true science. Boyle followed the ideas of the English scientist Francis Bacon (1561–1626), who said science should be based on experiment and observation. Many of the laboratory techniques Boyle developed were also used by Newton.

TIMELINE OF BREAKTHROUGHS 1600–1720

Newton acknowledged that his discoveries followed on from those made by earlier scientists around Europe. He lived during a period when scientific knowledge advanced rapidly, including these highlights:

1605 Johannes Kepler establishes his three Laws of Planetary Motion.

1608 Hans Lippershey invents a simple telescope.

1610 Galileo Galilei builds a telescope powerful enough to see the moons of Jupiter.

1633 René Descartes outlines his model of an **infinite** universe made of swirling whirlpools of fine matter.

1638 Galileo demonstrates that unequal weights fall at the same speed.

1642 Blaise Pascal invents an adding machine.

1656 Christiaan Huygens builds the first **pendulum** clock.

This coin celebrates the invention of the telescope.

1661 Robert Boyle publishes *The Sceptical Chymist*, which kickstarts the modern science of chemistry.

1664 Newton discovers that white light is made up of different colors.

1665 Robert Hooke uses the word **"cells"** to describe tiny chambers in living tissue he sees under a **microscope**.

1671 Newton completes his work on fluxions (it is not published until 1736).

1675 Newton argues that light is composed of particles.

1676 Ole Rømer makes the first estimate of the speed of light.

1684 Gottfried Leibniz publishes his invention of differential calculus.

1714 Daniel Fahrenheit constructs a mercury thermometer with a temperature scale.

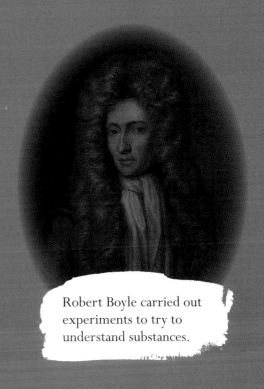

Robert Boyle carried out experiments to try to understand substances.

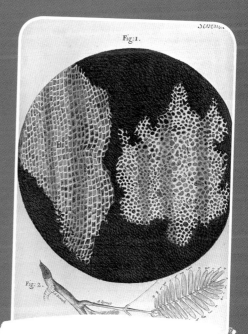

Robert Hooke made this drawing of the "cells" he saw when he studied leaves under a microscope.

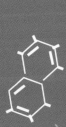
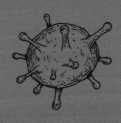
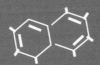

CHAPTER 3

Newton's discoveries helped to explain the relationship between sunlight and rainbows.

EXPERIMENTAL PHILOSOPHY
Breakthrough

Approach: The approach Newton took for his studies was René Descartes' idea of experimental philosophy, or using experimentation and mathematical equations to explain the laws of why things behaved as they did.

Method: Experimentation, observation, and hypothesis, repeated over and over again

Early breakthroughs: While he was still a student and junior professor, Newton achieved more than most scientists manage in a lifetime:

- Discovered gravity
- Invented a new form of math, today called calculus
- Discovered that white light is made of all the different colors put together
- Invented a **reflecting telescope**

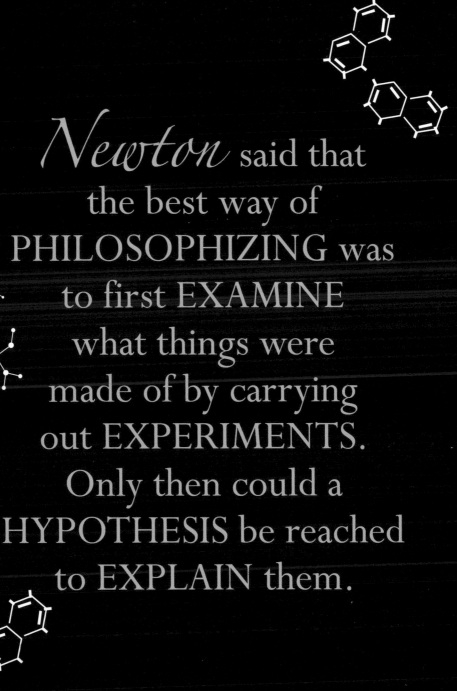

Newton said that the best way of PHILOSOPHIZING was to first EXAMINE what things were made of by carrying out EXPERIMENTS. Only then could a HYPOTHESIS be reached to EXPLAIN them.

INVESTIGATING LIGHT

In 1669, Newton became the new Lucasian Professor of Mathematics in Cambridge. It was a senior position he would hold for the next 24 years. He decided that his first lecture, or talk, would not be on mathematics but on optics, the study of light. Newton had been studying and experimenting with light since he was a young boy.

Scholars had debated the nature of light since the days of the ancient Greeks. Aristotle thought that, in its purest form, light was white. Newton disagreed, but he wanted to *prove* that Aristotle was wrong. While he was back at home in Lincolnshire during the plague, he happened to go to a country fair. There, he saw a set of **prisms**, or solid triangles of glass. He was fascinated by the way they seemed to break up the sunlight, so he bought them. Newton came up with an experiment.

He was fascinated by the way they seemed to break up the sunlight...

Newton uses a prism to study a beam of light entering a dark room.

He closed his window shutters so that just a tiny beam of sunlight could enter. As the light hit one side of the prism, it came out the other side as a rainbow: red, orange, yellow, green, blue, indigo, and violet. As the light passed through the prism, light of different colors was refracted, or bent, at different angles and so split into its different parts.

Ideas that changed the world

Newton wrote:"From what has been said it is also evident, that the whiteness of the Sun's light is compounded all the colours wherewith the several sorts of rays whereof that light consists, when by their several refrangibilities they are separated from one another, do tinge paper of any other white body whereon they fall."

Exploring the ideas

Newton's breakthrough was to realize that white light is made up of the colors of the rainbow. Descartes had claimed that white light was pure and unchanging, but that it changed color if it passed through another material. He never tested his theory. Newton's experiments showed he was wrong. To make sure, Newton set up two prisms. If Descartes was right, the colored light that passed through the second prism should change color again. Instead, red light refracted through the first prism stayed red after it went through the second. This proved to Newton that white light is made up of all the colors we can see.

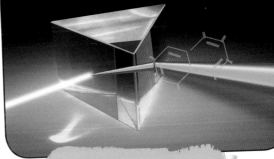

A prism bends different wavelengths of light by different amounts, making them scatter into bands of color.

HISTORY'S STORY

Newton sent the Royal Society a paper about his research into light. Founded in London in 1660, the Royal Society was a club of scholars (all men) who met to discuss science and do experiments. The society's motto was *Nullius in verba* ("Do not take anyone's word for anything"). Members believed the best way to advance knowledge was to challenge each other's ideas.

NEW TELESCOPE

Newton used his experiments with light to invent a telescope that was much smaller and more powerful than any telescope built before. Previous telescopes had passed light through lenses. Newton added a mirror inside the telescope to focus the light, creating the first reflecting telescope. He melted copper, tin, and poisonous arsenic to mold a mirror with the exact curve he needed. Newton's reflecting telescope gave a far clearer image than any previous device.

In 1675, King Charles II ordered the building of the Royal Observatory at Greenwich in London.

Newton's telescope caused a sensation. Despite being small enough to fit into someone's hand, the telescope could magnify objects almost 40 times. Soon, even King Charles II wanted to look at the night sky through Newton's telescope. In 1672, the Royal Society in London voted to make Newton one of its youngest-ever members.

The only problem with Newton's membership in the society was that he did not like sharing his ideas with other people. He did not want to discuss his ideas and hypotheses before he had figured them out for himself. He believed he knew better than any of his **contemporaries** how to solve the questions he posed, and he did not like to be questioned. If anybody challenged him, Newton often lost his temper.

This illustration shows Newton (seated, left) at a meeting of the Royal Society.

A nasty argument

One man who did disagree with Newton about the nature of light—and who spoke out strongly against him—was the famous natural philosopher Robert Hooke. While most of the members of the Royal Society agreed with Newton, Hooke argued that Newton's experiments did not prove what Newton claimed they did. Hooke said that Newton's paper was trying to say that light traveled in particles. Newton was furious: he said his paper did not say anything about how light traveled. It just proved the nature of white light.

The two men became locked in a **feud** that lasted for years. They insulted each other, accusing each other of stealing ideas, and became sworn enemies for life. Newton was so angry with Hooke that he decided that, from then on, he would not share his ideas with anyone and would go back to working on his own. He threatened to quit the Royal Society and only a large amount of flattery persuaded him to remain a member. Throughout Newton's life, he coped very badly whenever he felt threatened by other people's judgment or criticism. Some historians have wondered if Newton's insecurity grew in his childhood, when he felt lost and alone after he was sent to live with his grandparents.

THE MATH OF CHANGE

When Newton arrived at Cambridge University, algebra and geometry were the only types of math studied. He found both of them boring. Instead, he turned his attention to a new math that Descartes called "analytical geometry." It was a way of solving math problems in two or three **dimensions** rather than just on paper. Newton had found a subject that really excited him.

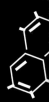

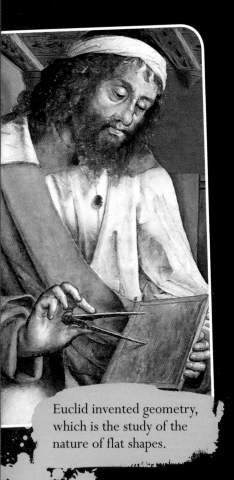

Euclid invented geometry, which is the study of the nature of flat shapes.

Newton taught himself Descartes' theories from his 1637 book *La Géométrie* (*Geometry*). Descartes' ideas were much more complex than those of the ancient Greek mathematician Euclid, who invented geometry around 300 B.C.E. Unfortunately for Newton, it was Euclid's geometry he had to know to pass his Cambridge examinations, and he was not very good at it. Fortunately for Newton, his friend Dr. Barrow passed him anyway.

While he was at home during the plague, Newton had a lot of time to ponder questions such as "How fast does a cannonball fly before it starts to fall?" and "Why do things always fall to Earth?" He was starting to think about motion. When he got back to Cambridge, he realized that math could help him answer these questions. He started to try to solve problems about moving objects. He called this new type of math "fluxions." Later, it became known as calculus.

A question of pride

Early in 1669, Isaac Barrow showed Newton a book that was causing a storm among math scholars in Europe. Written by the German mathematician Nicholas Mercator (c.1620–1687), it was a groundbreaking work that covered some of the same material that Newton had worked on while he was in Woolsthorpe. Newton realized that if he did not write down his ideas then, Mercator would be credited with having invented the new math.

Newton's calculus could explain the movement of a ball through the air—and his theory of gravity explained why it fell to Earth.

Newton showed his work, *De Analysi* (*Of Analyses*), to Barrow, who recognized it as a work of genius. Barrow persuaded Newton to send the work to John Collins, a London-based mathematician, who was in contact with all of Europe's leading mathematicians. Newton agreed, as long as his name was not on the manuscript. Collins copied out the paper and wrote to his fellow mathematicians about Newton's ideas. Soon, Newton's new math was the talk of math scholars across Europe.

Following fluxions

The basic principle of fluxions was that it used a series of equations to describe continuous motion. This gives a method of understanding how a value (such as the speed of a falling ball or the movement of a planet) changes over time. In addition, the equations can predict how an object will behave in the future. Today, calculus is used in fields such as science, engineering, medicine, and economics.

GREAT THINKERS OF THE AGE OF REASON

Newton knew and worked alongside some of the greatest scientists and thinkers of the age. However, his relationships with them were not always positive.

Isaac Barrow (1630–1677)

A math professor at Cambridge University, Barrow encouraged and recognized Newton's genius. He was instrumental in making math a subject of study at Cambridge. He came close to figuring out calculus.

Robert Boyle (1627–1691)

Boyle was one of the founding fathers of chemistry. He is most famous for Boyle's Law, which states that as the volume of a gas decreases, its pressure increases. Pressure is a measure of the force that a gas, or liquid, produces as it presses against its container. Working with Robert Hooke as his assistant, Boyle invented the air pump, which could create a **vacuum** by removing air from a chamber.

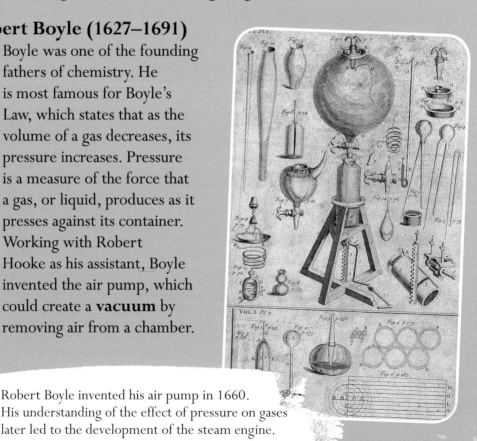

Robert Boyle invented his air pump in 1660. His understanding of the effect of pressure on gases later led to the development of the steam engine.

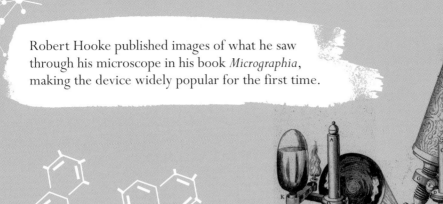

Robert Hooke published images of what he saw through his microscope in his book *Micrographia*, making the device widely popular for the first time.

Robert Hooke (1635–1703)

Best known for Hooke's Law, this natural philosopher stated that the force needed to stretch a spring increases with the distance it is stretched. His job was to carry out experiments at the Royal Society. He famously argued with Newton because he disagreed with the conclusions Newton drew from his own experiments. Hooke improved on the design of the newly invented microscope.

Nicholas Mercator (1620–1687)

When the German mathematician published his work on logarithms, it forced Newton into publishing his ideas about fluxions in *Of Analyses*. In its simplest form, a logarithm explains how many of one number we must multiply to make another number. For example, if the question is "How many 3s do we multiply to get 27?" the answer, or logarithm, is 3 ($3 \times 3 \times 3 = 27$).

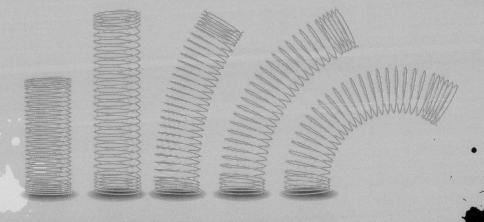

CHAPTER 4

Newton's theories explained why the planets remain in their orbits around the Sun.

SYSTEM OF THE UNIVERSE
Spreading Ideas

Newton's career spanned more than 20 years of scientific breakthroughs:

1666: During his "miraculous year," Newton starts to think about gravity.

1670s: Newton works on the math of gravity in Cambridge.

1674: Newton writes a paper that suggests the existence of "attractive powers," today known as gravity.

1684: He completes his calculations on gravity.

1685: He presents a paper about motion to the Royal Society.

1686: He completes the first volume of *Philosophiae Naturalis Principia Mathematica*.

1687: The three volumes of *Principia* are published, paid for by astronomer Edmond Halley.

Newton said that GRAVITY explains the MOTIONS of the planets, but it does not explain WHO or WHAT set the PLANETS in motion.

GRAVITY

Newton's return to Woolsthorpe during his university days set the course for his whole career. It gave him the thing he most wanted in the world: time. He sat and thought about the many questions he wanted to find answers to. Many of those questions arose from his advanced math calculations, which made him wonder about the forces at work in the universe.

According to legend, Newton was sitting under an apple tree one day when an apple fell. It suddenly occurred to him that a force must have attracted the apple toward the ground. Nobody knows whether this story is true, but Newton later used the example of an apple falling from a tree to try to explain the moon and how it is also attracted toward Earth.

Newton may have been inspired by an apple falling from a tree.

The apple that inspired Newton is one of the most famous pieces of fruit in history.

After years of thinking about the invisible force objects exert on each other in the form of gravity, Newton decided that it could be shown to be governed by what he called the Inverse Square Law. As two objects move away from each other, their gravitational pull on each other reduces by a set proportion. When one object is twice as far from the other object, the gravitational pull becomes one-fourth as strong.

Ideas that changed the world

Newton was once asked how he came up with his laws of gravity. His reply was simply, "By thinking about it all the time."

Exploring the ideas

Newton's ideas about gravity were based on earlier work. Johannes Kepler had argued that the planets travel around the Sun in **elliptical** rather than circular orbits. This was accepted at that time. But no one could explain it until Newton's ideas about gravity explained how the Sun's pull on the planets depended on their distance from it. The Inverse Square Law provided the math that explained the forces that linked the Sun and planets in the solar system. Newton's Law of Universal Gravitation explained that Earth, the moon, the planets, and stars all moved according to the same principle: gravity. The math that showed how invisible gravity worked also offered an explanation as to the whole shape of the universe.

The force that makes a tree's apples fall is the same as the force that holds the moon in place in the sky.

HISTORY'S STORY

Newton calculated that the moon was 60 times further from the center of Earth than the apple. Using his Inverse Square Law, he calculated the force of the attraction between the moon and Earth as a rate of $1/3{,}600$ of the speed of the apple's fall, so Earth's pull on the apple was 3,600 times stronger than its pull on the moon (60 x 60 = 3,600).

35

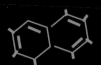

LAWS OF MOTION

The astronomer Edmond Halley (1656–1742) was Newton's great friend. Halley realized his friend was a genius, but it took all his persuasion to get Newton to write down his theories. He wanted Newton to go public with his proof that planets move in elliptical orbits. Finally, Newton sent off a short paper, *De Motu* (*On Motion*), to the Royal Society in 1685.

The paper was the first step toward writing down 20 years' worth of ideas about how the universe came together. Newton set out definitions for the natural world that are still used today:

Matter is anything that takes up space, while **mass** is the amount of matter. Momentum is the quantity of motion of a moving thing, which is the product of speed and mass. **Inertia** is the way that an object that is resting or moving will continue in the same state unless it is affected by an external force. Force is an action applied on a body, and centripetal force is an attraction toward the center of something. These terms would be important for the next step Newton took.

Edmond Halley gave his name to Halley's **comet**, which he predicted would return to Earth every 75 years.

Laws of Motion

Using his definitions, Newton set down three laws that govern all motion. In doing so, he laid the foundations for the subject of physics. His three laws were:

1. **The Law of Inertia.** An object in motion will stay in motion unless it is acted upon by an outside force. An object at rest stays at rest unless it is acted upon by an outside force.

2. **The Law of Acceleration.** The rate at which the speed of an object changes is **proportional** to the force acting on it.

3. **The Law of Action and Reaction.** For every action, there is an equal and opposite reaction.

A mechanistic universe

The three Laws of Motion were a completely new way to explain the universe. Most people still viewed the world in the same way as their medieval ancestors. They thought that the planets and stars moved thanks to God. Newton did not contradict this. He said he did not know what had started the planets moving—but that the way they moved could be explained by math. Just like the workings of a machine, the actions of the universe could be measured and counted.

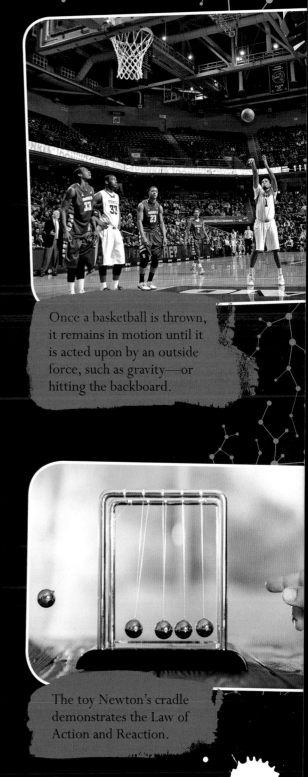

Once a basketball is thrown, it remains in motion until it is acted upon by an outside force, such as gravity—or hitting the backboard.

The toy Newton's cradle demonstrates the Law of Action and Reaction.

SYSTEM OF THE WORLD

When Newton presented his short paper to the Royal Society in 1685, its members were very excited. They knew that Newton's ideas were groundbreaking. Halley begged Newton to expand his work. Newton agreed and went on to produce one of the greatest scientific books in history, *Philosophiae Naturalis Principia Mathematica* (*Mathematical Principles of Natural Philosophy*), known as *Principia* for short.

In *Principia*, Newton explained the shape of the universe using math and the laws he had figured out. The book was the sum of all Newton's thinking and study. Once he had set out his definitions and defined the three Laws of Motion, Newton set out his greatest idea of all: the Law of Universal Gravitation.

This illustration of Newton was made by the poet and artist William Blake in 1795. It shows Newton using a compass to measure shapes.

He described how everything in the universe obeyed the same laws, and included the math that proved how gravity worked. The book showed, once and for all, that Aristotle's teaching, which the world had followed for 2,000 years, was wrong. Earth did not operate according to a different set of rules than the Sun, moon, planets, and stars. They all operated according to the same set of rules. Gravity was the invisible force that held the universe together.

Simple…or not so simple

Newton's detailed account showed that the universe actually functioned in a simple way. The book marked the high point in Newton's thinking. He spent the next 20 years refining his thoughts and revising the three volumes of *Principia*. The Royal Society agreed to publish the first volume in 1686, but had run out of funds. Halley offered to pay for the publication of all three volumes. When *Principia* was published in the summer of 1687, Newton became the most famous scientist in Europe.

Since its publication, every scientist has based their ideas on Newton's book. The book, although it contained a simple idea, was so hard to follow that most people could not understand it. Newton had deliberately made it hard to understand because he did not want to waste time answering stupid questions!

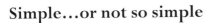

Halley's comet appears in the Bayeux Tapestry, about the invasion of England by the Normans in 1066.

HISTORY'S STORY

A mathematician and astronomer, Edmond Halley figured out that comets do not travel in straight lines. By studying accounts of past comets, he figured out that comets in 1531, 1607, and 1682 were actually the same comet. From this, he was able to predict when the same comet would reappear: 1758. When the comet reappeared on cue, it was named for Halley.

NEWTON'S KEY WORKS

Method of Fluxions (1671)
Only published after Newton's death in 1736, this was a complete account of his theory of calculus.

Philosophiae Naturalis Principia Mathematica (1687)
Known as *Principia* for short, this was Newton's masterwork. It set down his three Laws of Motion and his Law of Universal Gravitation.

Opticks: or, A Treatise of the Reflexions, Refractions, Inflexions and Colours of Light (1704)
This work contained Newton's analysis of the fundamental nature of light by means of the refraction of light by prisms and lenses, as well as the **diffraction** of light by closely spaced sheets of glass.

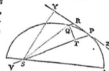

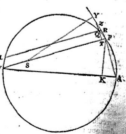

This page from Newton's *Principia* shows mathematical problems relating to sections of an arc or circle.

Newton's *Chronology* attempted to tie in biblical events such as the building of the Tower of Babel with recorded history.

The Queries (1704–1718)

This was the third part of *Opticks* and answered questions that the book had raised. Newton added to it and expanded on it for 14 years. The book also gave his thoughts on the future questions science would raise.

The Chronology of Ancient Kingdoms Amended (1728)

This 87,000-word work was published after Newton's death. It was not a science book but an attempt to get the biblical account of the ancient past to align with historical sources about ancient times.

CHAPTER 5

This statue of Newton was commissioned for the chapel at Trinity College, Cambridge, in 1755.

A FAMOUS MAN
Reputation

These are some of the honors given to Newton during his lifetime:

1669: Appointed Lucasian Professor of Mathematics at the University of Cambridge

1689: Elected as Member of Parliament for the University of Cambridge

1699: Made an Associate of the French Académie des Sciences

1699: Appointed Master of the Royal Mint, where coins were made

1703: Elected President of the Royal Society

1705: Knighted (giving him the honorary title "sir") by Queen Anne, making him the second scientist to be knighted, after Sir Francis Bacon

1714: Made a Commissioner of the Board of Longitude, which aimed to find a way of pinpointing a ship's east–west position while at sea, using imaginary lines running from north to south around the globe

Newton once said that to explain ALL of NATURE was too difficult a task for any ONE MAN and even for any ONE AGE.

NEW DIRECTION

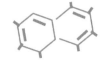

The publication of *Principia* made Newton one of the most famous men in Europe. He was so famous in England that he was elected to the English Parliament to represent the University of Cambridge. However, Newton's growing fame also largely marked the end of his scientific career.

Newton decided he had had enough of life in Cambridge. He had held the position of Lucasian Professor of Math for 24 years and now he wanted a change by moving to London. Among his new friends in London was the famous diary-writer Samuel Pepys (1633–1703). Pepys was then the president of the Royal Society.

With his future unclear…Newton fell into a deep depression.

London life was busy, and the more time Newton spent there, the more he realized he would need a well-paid position to afford the kind of house he wanted and to pay for servants. With his future unclear and exhausted by 20 years of solid work, Newton fell into a deep depression in early 1693. Some historians think this breakdown may also have been the result of the sudden end of Newton's very close friendship with the Swiss mathematician Nicolas Fatio de Duillier.

When Newton started to feel better, he worked on a revised *Principia*, answering questions other scientists had asked him. Finally, in 1696, he got the job he wanted when the government made him Warden of the Royal Mint in the Tower of London. The Royal Mint was responsible for making all England's gold and silver coins. The post came with a large salary. After three and a half years as Warden, Newton became Master of the Mint.

Ideas that changed the world

Newton wrote: "**Atheism** is so senseless. When I look at the solar system, I see the Earth at the right distance from the Sun to receive the proper amounts of heat and light. This did not happen by chance."

Exploring the ideas

All his life, Newton was a sincere and dedicated Christian who read the Bible every day. He believed that his discoveries of order and planning within the universe were proof that a greater being had planned it. He did not think that his theories and laws proved that God did not exist—quite the opposite.

This coin was made at the Royal Mint during the reign of Queen Anne.

The Royal Mint was in the Tower of London. Newton took his job so seriously that he hung out in bars in disguise to catch forgers.

HISTORY'S STORY

For years before Newton became Warden of the Royal Mint, **counterfeiters** had been forging coins or melting down their gold and silver and replacing them with cheaper metals. Since England's economy was based on how much gold and silver it had (including in its coins), this was a problem. Newton set about making the coins impossible to copy.

SPIRITUAL PURSUITS

As well as being a committed Christian, Newton had many other interests that he followed with the same dedication and single-mindedness as he pursued his math and science. He spent many years studying **alchemy** and **prophecy**.

Alchemists were seen as being more like magicians than like modern scientists.

Newton kept a private laboratory at Trinity College where he built himself a pair of furnaces to heat the ingredients he used in his experiments. No one was allowed in except his great friend John Wickins. This was because Newton was practicing alchemy, or trying to turn one substance into another. Alchemy was illegal. The Church said that alchemy was a sin and punished anyone caught practicing it. For a Christian such as Newton, this was a strange interest.

*Alchemists thought they could create a magical…"**elixir** of life."*

Alchemy can be traced as far back as the ancient Babylonians and Egyptians. It was an early form of chemistry. Alchemists wanted to turn common metals, such as lead, into precious metals such as silver or gold, using a mystical substance called the "philosopher's stone." As well as trying to make gold, alchemists thought they could create a magical liquid called the "elixir of life." In his experimenting, Newton approached this half-magical pursuit with the same dedication he gave to figuring out how the universe functioned. He wrote more than a million words about alchemy.

Predicting the future

The time that Newton lived in was one of great change. Science was in its early days, and the power of the Church remained strong. **Protestantism** was the new religion in England, and its followers were just as **devout** as those who followed the Catholic faith it had replaced. Most people were superstitious and took events such as the plague and the Great Fire of London in 1666 as signs that the world was ending and that Jesus Christ would soon return to Earth for his Second Coming. The 1680 comet was taken as another sign of approaching doom.

Amid all that confusion, Newton tried to make sense of his religion and the world he lived in. He had some highly personal beliefs, such as believing that, although Jesus was the Son of God, he was not God's equal. Newton took the Bible literally and tried to link the different prophecies he read in the Books of Daniel and Revelations with historical events. He even persuaded a friend to write a book predicting when the Second Coming would happen—although he was never willing to give a date!

The Great Fire of London burned for five days in September 1666. It destroyed most of the medieval part of the city, including more than 13,000 homes.

AMBITION AND ARGUMENTS

Newton was still attending meetings at the Royal Society. In fact, he had an ambitious new plan: He wanted to be president of the society. When the current holder of the position, his old enemy Robert Hooke, died in 1703, he started trying to persuade people that he was the best man for the job.

The person nominated for the post of president was Sir Christopher Wren (1632–1723), the architect who had designed the new St. Paul's Cathedral after the old building was destroyed by the Great Fire. However, Wren generously turned down the position in favor of Newton, who, he said, was the better scientist. Newton decided the society was in need of change. During Hooke's leadership, Newton felt it had lost its way.

Hooke was also a bad-tempered person who, some people claimed, had used his position as president to take credit for others' ideas. Once he was president, Newton made sure that he surrounded himself with people who would agree with him. However, his oversensitive and controlling personality soon took over, driving some of his friends away.

Christopher Wren designed St. Paul's Cathedral with its famous dome, which was considered a marvel of engineering.

Arguments and more arguments

In 1704, Newton finally published his version of calculus, which he had invented years earlier. An anonymous review suggested that Newton might have stolen his ideas from a German mathematician named Gottfried Leibniz (1646–1716). Newton was extremely angry. He did not want anyone to get the credit for inventing calculus except himself, and he accused Leibniz of stealing his ideas. The two men were soon locked in an ugly fight.

Finally, in 1711, Leibniz asked the Royal Society to settle the matter once and for all. This was a mistake. As president, Newton not only put himself in charge of the committee that looked into the matter, he also wrote its report. When the report was published in 1713, unsurprisingly, it suggested that Leibniz had indeed stolen Newton's ideas.

Gottfried Leibniz was a mathematical genius who came up with his ideas on calculus in around 1675.

HISTORY'S STORY

Gottfried Leibniz published his paper on calculus in 1684. For a while, he had exchanged friendly letters with Newton about their discoveries. Later, Newton was determined to beat Leibniz and had no regrets about his behavior toward the other man, even though Leibniz died heartbroken after the society's findings.

49

NEWTON'S QUARRELS

Newton was known for his bad temper and his readiness to hold a grudge. He argued with many of the leading scholars of the day:

Newton versus Leibniz

Gottfried Leibniz started working on his theory of calculus around the same time as Newton, in 1675. Newton's reluctance to make his work public until he was certain there were no errors meant that Leibniz published his paper first, in 1684. When Newton finally published his paper in 1704, there was a suggestion that he had copied Leibniz. Newton was furious. As president of the Royal Society, he wrote a report that said Leibniz had copied him. The ruling destroyed Leibniz, who never recovered. Newton claimed he was happy to have hastened Leibniz toward his death.

Newton versus Hooke

Hooke carried out experiments for the Royal Society. When he questioned the conclusions Newton had drawn from his light experiments, the two men argued. Hooke actually agreed with a lot of what Newton said but, by questioning Newton, he earned his fury. The two men remained enemies for life but, in public, they pretended they had resolved their differences. Newton even went as far as to admit he was very grateful for Hooke's work.

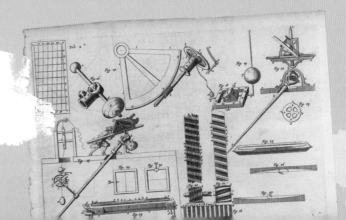

Robert Hooke was a talented inventor who improved the telescope and came up with other optical instruments.

Newton versus Flamsteed

John Flamsteed (1646–1719) was the Astronomer Royal, a position created by King Charles II, at the Royal Observatory in Greenwich. There, he gathered a huge catalog of data tracking the movement of the Sun, moon, planets, and stars. During the 1690s, Newton repeatedly asked Flamsteed for his data to use for his own research, but Flamsteed did not want to share his work before he had a chance to publish it. It was only when Newton became president of the Royal Society that he had the authority to force Flamsteed to publish some of his data. Flamsteed was furious, but kept on charting the night sky and eventually had the last laugh. In 1725, after Flamsteed's death, two of Flamsteed's assistants published a vast account of Flamsteed's work, for which he is rightly famous.

John Flamsteed cataloged the position of more than 3,000 stars.

The clouds in this photo of the distant universe are huge nurseries where new stars are being created.

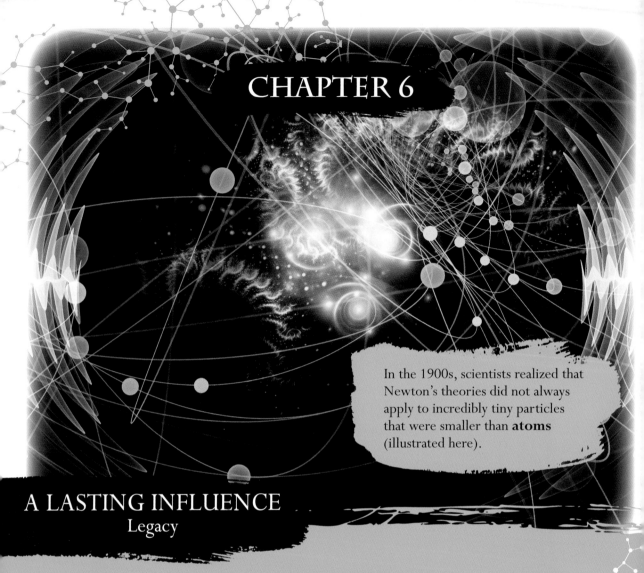

CHAPTER 6

In the 1900s, scientists realized that Newton's theories did not always apply to incredibly tiny particles that were smaller than **atoms** (illustrated here).

A LASTING INFLUENCE
Legacy

Newton's career laid the foundations for a century of scientific discoveries:

1780s: Antoine Lavoisier discovers the Law of Conservation of Mass, which states that mass cannot be created or destroyed, although it may change its form or position.

1801: Thomas Young proves his theory that light travels as waves. It is not until the 1900s that scientists discover light can also behave completely differently, like particles.

1803: John Dalton proposes that matter is made up of tiny units called atoms.

1829: Gaspard-Gustave de Coriolis figures out the math relating to kinetic energy, which is the energy that an object has as a result of its motion.

1843: James Prescott Joule studies heat and its relationship with work and energy, leading to the Law of the Conservation of Energy. This states that energy cannot be created or destroyed, but can change form.

Newton believed there was no higher source of EARTHLY HONOR or distinction than that connected with ADVANCES in SCIENCE.

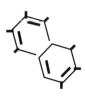

LEADING TO REVOLUTION

In 1705, Newton was knighted by Queen Anne. With his mind still sharp, he carried on working until shortly before his death on March 20, 1727. Newton was the first scientist to be given the honor of a burial in London's Westminster Abbey, where only monarchs and leading Englishmen were buried.

Soon after his death, Newton, along with Galileo and Robert Boyle, became popular with a group of forward-thinking philosophers. Their ideas soon spread across Europe. Today, this period in history is known as the Age of Reason or the Enlightenment. The most famous philosophers of the age included the Frenchman Voltaire (1694–1778) and Englishman John Locke (1632–1704). Using Newton's laws of gravity and motion, these philosophers argued that everything in the universe could be understood by reason, or what they called "natural law."

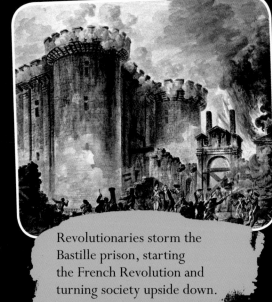

Revolutionaries storm the Bastille prison, starting the French Revolution and turning society upside down.

These philosophers dismissed the idea that God had created the world with a fixed order. They used reason to challenge everything. This led to new attitudes far beyond science: people started to question why society was based on the idea that the king was a representative of God on Earth. Their ideas about freedom and equality eventually led to the French Revolution (1789–1799) and American Revolution (1765–1783).

Ideas that changed the world

Newton wrote: "Tis much better to do a little with certainty, and leave the rest for others that come after you, than to explain all things by **conjecture** *without making sure of any thing."*

Exploring the ideas

Throughout his long life, Newton observed, experimented, thought, and questioned again and again. He left long periods of time between his discoveries and publishing his findings, because he wanted to be certain that his theories were correct. Always a loner, Newton did not welcome working together with other scientists. He wanted his ideas to be his alone. In his view, it was better to make small breakthroughs on which other scientists could build in future generations than to make sweeping statements, like Aristotle and Descartes, that would later be found to be wrong.

Newton's monument in Westminster Abbey was erected in 1731. It describes him as having a mind that was "almost divine."

HISTORY'S STORY

One of the key works of the Age of Reason was the *Encyclopédie*, published in France between 1751 and 1772. The work had 17 volumes written by leading thinkers. Its aim was "to change the way people think" by giving everyone access to the most modern knowledge. Its chief scientific editor, Jean le Ronde d'Alembert, praised Newton for shaping the Age of Reason.

NEW ROMANTICS

By the beginning of the 1800s, a new movement had begun to take hold in Europe, in opposition to the Age of Reason. The Romantic movement rejected the idea that reason was the basis of the world, including Newton's idea of a universe in which everything could be explained. Romanticism was most popular between 1800 and 1850, as the **Industrial Revolution** took off in England, Europe, and North America.

The Romantic movement was powered by artists, writers, poets, and musicians who rejected the idea of a rational, ordered universe. Instead, they embraced the imagination and said that **irrationality** and emotion were more important than reason. Rather than work together, Romantics prized the individual's achievements and experiences. They saw themselves as heroes and heroines of their generation, whom the rest of society followed. They lived their lives according to their own rules, which were generally seen as shocking by more conventional members of society.

Freeing the imagination

Above everything, the Romantics saw the imagination as being the most important human quality. They also prized wild and natural landscapes over the growing cities and new factories that came with the Industrial Revolution.

The Romantics' awe of nature is expressed in Caspar David Friedrich's painting of a traveler in the mountains.

The Romantic movement produced many great works of art, such as the poems of the English poets Lord Byron and William Wordsworth. Wordsworth described a statue of Newton in his poem "The Prelude," with "his prism and silent face." The German artist Caspar David Friedrich meanwhile claimed that "the artist's feeling is his law."

Frankenstein

The English writer Mary Shelley's novel *Frankenstein* (1823) told the story of a scientist who creates a monster during an experiment. It summed up the Romantics' fear of where modern science might lead. Many scientists of the first half of the 1800s did not want to abandon the methods of Galileo and Newton. They did, however, emphasize that nature could be freer from rules than scientists such as Newton suggested. They argued that it was only through emotional appreciation that humans could understand nature.

Today, these two opposing views of nature, as something to be controlled by science or something that must be allowed its freedom, are still being fought over. Perhaps, today, they are even more relevant than ever before.

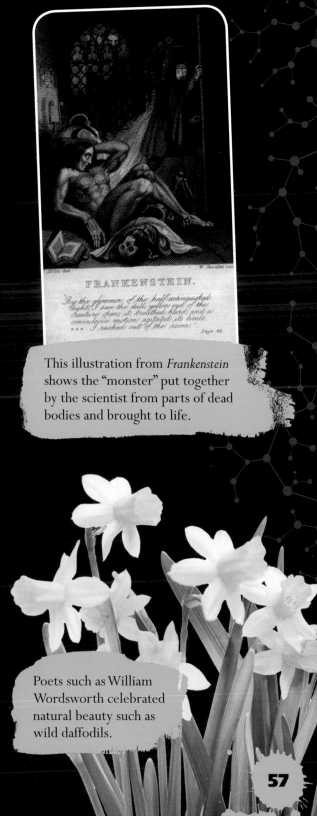

This illustration from *Frankenstein* shows the "monster" put together by the scientist from parts of dead bodies and brought to life.

Poets such as William Wordsworth celebrated natural beauty such as wild daffodils.

A NEW PHYSICS

Newton's laws of motion and gravity governed how scientists saw the universe until the beginning of the 1900s. For centuries after his death, it had seemed that Newton had discovered all the important laws of physics. As the 1900s began, however, it soon became clear that this was not the case. Physicists such as Albert Einstein (1879–1955) took physics in new directions that required new laws.

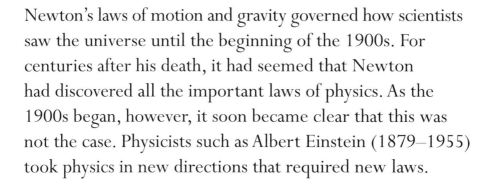

Newton's laws could not explain certain new **phenomena** that had been discovered since his death—and are still being discovered today. Newton had proven that much of the universe worked in an ordered structure. But today, we know that order contains many levels of seeming **randomness** that still require explanation and understanding.

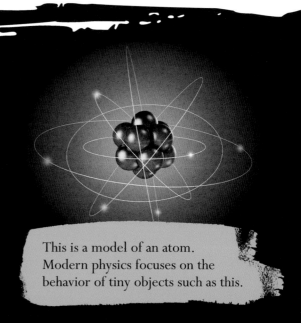

This is a model of an atom. Modern physics focuses on the behavior of tiny objects such as this.

The realization that new laws would be needed led to the modern era of physics, which is known as post-Newtonian physics. Newton's physics, which is now known as classical physics, had dealt with nature on an observable scale, or what we can actually see. The new physics needed to describe objects whose existence was only a theory. Newton's physics concentrated on relatively low speeds and large distances. In contrast, modern physics looks at tiny distances and much greater speeds, such as the movement of particles within an atom, which are beyond Newton's old laws.

Smaller and faster

Physicists in the 1900s explored ideas that were more and more theoretical, or unproven. Max Planck (1858–1947) explored the idea that light was both a particle and a wave of energy at the same time. Einstein explored what happened to objects traveling near the speed of light. Werner Heisenberg (1901–1976) developed quantum mechanics, which is about how tiny particles such as atoms and parts of atoms behave.

The Uncertainty Principle

Heisenberg's Uncertainty Principle stated that, at such a small level, the certainties of Newton's laws did not apply. It was possible to know either the position of an atom or its speed—but not both at the same time. This raised the mind-bending possibility that an atom could be in two places at one time. Such developments showed that, while Newton's theories are true for much of the universe, a new set of laws is needed to understand atoms, as well as how space and time operate.

MAX PLANCK

The work of later physicists such as Max Planck led to the development of quantum mechanics, which studies the behavior of particles smaller than atoms.

HISTORY'S STORY

The Danish physicist Niels Bohr (1885–1962) worked on the structure of the atom and quantum physics. He came up with the idea of "complementarity"— that items could have contradictory, or seemingly impossible, properties at the same time. For example, he studied how particles could behave like a wave and like a stream of particles—both at once!

NEWTON'S POSTHUMOUS HONORS

Places and Things
Since his death, Newton has had many objects, ideas, and places named after him, including:

8000 Isaac Newton, an asteroid that orbits the Sun in our solar system's Asteroid Belt

Newton numbers, also known as kissing numbers, which are defined as the number of equally sized balls that can touch a central ball (clue: in one dimension, the answer is 2, because one circle can touch the central circle on either side, but the number increases by adding extra dimensions...)

Newton's cradle, a popular desktop toy that shows how Newton's Laws of Motion work

Newton's tree, a 360-year-old apple tree at his family home of Woolsthorpe Manor, Lincolnshire, England

Newtontoppen, a mountain on the island of Spitsbergen, Norway, one of the most northerly inhabited places in the world

This apple tree at Woolsthorpe is claimed to be where Newton saw the apple fall—but there is doubt that the event actually happened.

This statue of Newton by Eduardo Paolozzi, which was based on a drawing by William Blake (see page 38). It was created for the piazza of the British Library.

Where to See Newton

Monument at Westminster Abbey, London, England, erected to him in 1731

Statue with apple, at Oxford University Museum of Natural History, England, carved by Alexander Munro in 1860

Statue with dividers, at the British Library, London, England, carved by Eduardo Paolozzi in 1995

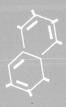

On the British £1 banknote, between 1978 and 1988

GLOSSARY

Age of Reason A European movement of the seventeenth and eighteenth centuries (1600s and 1700s) that emphasized reason, or logical thought

alchemy An early form of chemistry, often trying to turn common metals into gold

algebra A branch of mathematics in which letters and symbols are used to represent numbers

astronomers People who study the stars, planets, and space

atheism Lack of belief in a god

atoms The smallest parts of matter that can exist independently

bacteria Tiny living things that can cause disease

calculus A branch of mathematics that deals with defining change

cells The smallest parts of any living thing

chemistry The branch of science that studies the characteristics of substances

comet A rocky, icy body that travels through the solar system

conclusion A judgment reached by reasoning

conjecture An opinion formed on the basis of not enough information

contagious Spread from one being to another

contemporaries People living at the same time

counterfeiters People who make a copy of something with the aim of fraud

data Facts collected for study

devout Having deep religious feelings

diffraction The process by which a beam of light is spread out

dimensions Measurements in a particular direction, such as height, length, or width

elixir A magical potion

elliptical Oval

equations Mathematical statements that say two things are equal

feud A long and bitter disagreement

fundamental Of basic importance

geometry A branch of mathematics that deals with shape, size, and position

gravity The force that pulls all objects toward each other

house arrest Being kept a prisoner in one's own house

hypothesis A possible explanation for observed facts, given as a starting point for investigation

Industrial Revolution The period between 1760 and 1840 when new inventions led to the development of machine tools and factories

inertia The tendency to do nothing or stay the same

infinite Without end

interactions Effects on each other

irrationality Not being logical or reasonable

logic A reasonable way of thinking, based on good judgment

mass Weight

matter Any physical substance

mechanical philosophy A field of study that sees the universe as a vast and complex machine

microscope An instrument used to magnify tiny objects

natural philosophy An old term used to describe the study of nature and the universe, before the development of modern science

observatory A building that houses a telescope for studying space

optics The study of sight and the behavior of light

orbited Moved around the Sun, or another body, in a curved path

particles Tiny pieces of matter

pendulum A weight on a string that swings freely

phenomena Facts or situations that are observed to exist

philosophy The study of large questions, such as the nature of life and the universe

physics The branch of science concerned with the nature and properties of matter and energy

plague A disease caused by bacteria passed to humans from black rats and fleas

posthumous After death

prism A triangular-shaped piece of solid glass

prophecy A prediction of the future

proportional Corresponding in size to something else

Protestantism A branch of Christianity

randomness State of lacking a pattern or organization

reflecting telescope A telescope in which a mirror is used to collect and focus light

undergraduate A university student who has not completed their first degree

vacuum A space completely without matter

FOR MORE INFORMATION

BOOKS

Coates, Eileen S. *Isaac Newton and the Laws of Motion* (STEM Milestones: Historic Inventions and Discoveries). New York, NY: PowerKids Press, 2019.

Meyer, Susan. *Isaac Newton* (Leaders of the Scientific Revolution). New York, NY: Rosen Young Adult, 2017.

Tolish, Alexander. *Gravity Explained* (The Mysteries of Space). New York, NY: Enslow Publishing, 2018.

Wood, Alix. *Isaac Newton* (World-Changing Scientists). New York, NY: PowerKids Press, 2019.

WEBSITES

Biography—www.ducksters.com/biography/scientists/isaac_newton.php
A website with information about Newton's life.

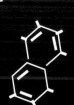

Gravity—spaceplace.nasa.gov/what-is-gravity/en
A detailed description of gravity and its effect on the shape of the universe.

Laws of Motion—www.physics4kids.com/files/motion_laws.html
A clear summary of Newton's three Laws of Motion and what they mean in real life.

Timeline—https://bit.ly/2vHHQgk
A detailed timeline of Newton's life and work, including his major discoveries.

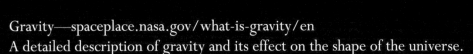

INDEX

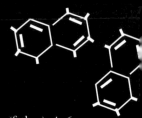